EGO @WORK

HANS BEGEER / ROEL H. REITZEMA

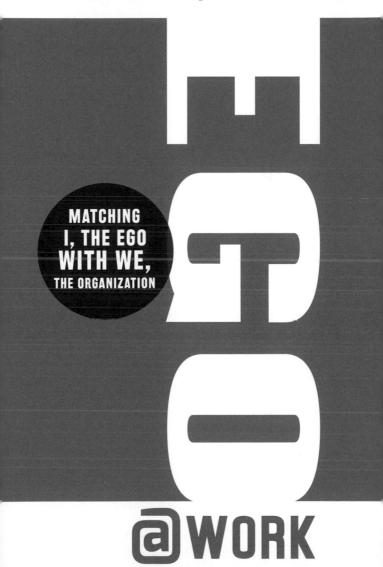

EGO

MATCHING I, THE EGO WITH WE, THE ORGANIZATION

@WORK

This book was originally published as *Ego@WORK*, LannooCampus, 2019.

D/2020/45/146 – ISBN 978 94 014 6825 1 – NUR 807, 808

Cover and interior design: Gert Degrande | De Witlofcompagnie
Translation: Lynn Butler

LannooCampus Publishers is a subsidiary of Lannoo Publishers,
the book and multimedia division of Lannoo Publishers nv.

LannooCampus Publishers

Vaartkom 41 box 01.02   P.O. Box 23202
3000 Leuven   1100 DS Amsterdam
Belgium   Netherlands
www.lannoocampus.com

Sometimes my ego shouts at me, it tells me what to do
It builds me up or tears me down
It helps me yet it hurts me as it pushes me around

Sometimes it whispers softly, so softly I can't tell
It makes me act like such a fool
Makes me lash out and be quite cruel

Sometimes I stop my ego from getting in my way
Then others' thoughts and hopes and words
Can touch my soul, be really heard

Sometimes my ego balances with others in my life
Our egos then mesh beautifully
We work together fruitfully

With time I know I'll find the path to ego virtuosity
My ego as an instrument
Finely tuned, my implement
To build a better life

(Lynn Butler)

CONTENTS

WITH
PRACTICAL
MODEL
P. 38 & 41

1

WHY SHOULD YOU READ THIS BOOK?

You probably don't think about your ego very often. Do you have any idea how your ego comes across to other people? Did you know that 95% of your behavior is driven by your unconscious mind? Can you apply your conscious mind to manage yourself better?

When we talk about the ego, it is often in a negative sense: "A really big ego just entered the room; he is so self-centered!" But what is an ego? The ego is the instrument through which you develop your behavior. Your ego has made choices for you over the course of your life, from your infancy through your childhood, education and work experiences.

We are unaware of most of these choices, but they influence our behavior. Today, everything we do must be done quickly, we must identify problems and fix them immediately. As a result, we don't take enough time to consider our options. We act almost without thinking, driven by our ego, on autopilot. This is true of almost everyone. Groups of people who must work together have to deal with many egos. When everyone reacts automatically, driven by their egos, collisions and conflicts result and efficiency suffers.

How can we get to know more about our ego and how it determines our behavior? This can be done through introspection and by contemplating the feedback of others. It is in our interest to adjust our own ego so that we can evolve to a point where we are aware of our ego and manage it to make choices from an inclusive (We) rather than an egocentric (I) perspective. The focus of this book is to help us become more aware of our ego, to provide techniques to evolve from I to We thinking and to facilitate harmony and improve efficiency in the workplace.

Each topic in this book is presented from the perspective of I and We. After reading this book, you will have answers to the following questions:

From the I-perspective:
• How do I develop more ego-awareness or consciousness?

- How does positive ego-development contribute to more authenticity?
- How can I overcome defense mechanisms of the ego?
- How can I increase my creativity and problem-solving capacity?
- How can I develop new behavior?

From the We-perspective:
- Which leadership competencies do you have, that will enable you to develop more ethical and social skills?
- What new authority do you have to develop and how can you get rid of the old authority?
- What kind of new social contracts are needed?
- Which roles and processes fit these?
- How do you grow spiritual presence?

The book is structured as follows:
- In chapters 2-4, we describe what ego is about and how it manifests itself.
- In chapters 5-9, we develop and present our model.
- In chapter 10, we describe a case study to illustrate the use of our model.
- In chapter 11, we discuss lessons from the book.
- In chapter 12, we advise how this book can be of help to you.

We interviewed business leaders from a range of sectors in Belgium and the Netherlands on the topic of ego at the workplace. Their combined views together with our experience in the field of management consulting and training constitute this book. Excerpts from the interviews appear throughout the book, with the initials of the interviewees appearing between brackets.

2

THE EGO AS AN ANTHOLOGY
OF WHO WE ARE

QUOTES FROM BUSINESS LEADERS – SNAPSHOTS OF
THE EGO IN THE WORKPLACE

The word "ego" is defined by most dictionaries in mostly negative terms such as egocentric, egoism, egotistic, ego trip, and so on. We found the same thing in our consultancy work and in interviews conducted for this book. But when we probed more deeply, we found that strong ego, nevertheless, is deemed necessary to drive changes in the workplace. Interviewees also believed that ego development can be beneficial. Our interviewees see ego as an anthology, a collection of the different facets of our personalities. In this chapter, we present quotes from the interviews.

WHAT COMES TO MIND WHEN
YOU THINK OF EGO IN THE WORKPLACE?

Ego is seen too often as negative, as an obstacle,
as a distraction. But a strong ego can help people
to be more authentic, to have more respect for
themselves and for others. **(BDB)**

Leaders without vanity, without ego, don't exist.
Leaders need to rule the pack, to be
the alpha animal. **(JMD)**

I don't see myself standing above my team, but my team
does. My challenge is to stay in line with my team –
not too far ahead nor lagging behind. **(HW)**

I care for my employees and I expect them to
care for our company. **(IGe)**

Ego is powerful and destructive. Dominant, limited,
all about survival, ego is often in a childish,
infantile state. **(NB)**

Everybody has the right to have a strong ego but
they must take care that their egos evolve enough to
be manageable. **(RV)**

Big egos are characterized by a blue suit and brown shoes,
people who talk a lot and listen little and who are looking
solely for promotions. **(SVU)**

Environments that accept egos are characterized by security, openness, inclusiveness and acceptance of differences.
As long as the egos don't feel threatened, these are the
environments that promote growth. **(AVP)**

Employees of today have a low tolerance for big egos and
egotistic behavior. They will protest against people with big
egos if necessary. **(TS)**

Ego is simply a mental concept, a state of mind.
If I look for my ego, I find nothing. (RH)

Open environments are needed to develop the ego.
Show trust by involving people in taking difficult
decisions, show vulnerability. (MH)

Ego does not improve the quality of life; rather,
it restrains one from being happy. Ego is a form of
self-defense; it masks our true selves. (ME)

Ego is the essence of a person, the fundamental
nature combining our heart and our soul. Our ego
determines how we feel and behave. (TL)

Believing in ego is like believing in God. We humans
need something to ground us, something to believe.
Identification with this gives us energy and drive.
But egos can be dangerous. (IGo)

My experience with ego is that it overwhelms us and
makes us resistant and inflexible and unable to share.
This reduces opportunities for participation from others.
Big egos create submissiveness in others.
Ego strives to retain any power given to it
by the organization and becomes narcissistic. **(SJ)**

Ego gets in the way of the leaders. They tend to think
of themselves as the center of the universe, they behave
selfishly. Narcissism leads them to look inward and lose
touch with their environment. **(LdV)**

Ego is about individuality, identity. What makes me, me?
What is my character like, how do I respond in different
situations and why? What do I offer as a leader?
This is a constellation of positives and negatives and
it is often subconscious. **(MV)**

ILLUSTRATION OF THE POWER OF EGO:

Ego determines our identity and gives us power.
Your ego illustrates your colors. **(AVP)**

Ego stimulates listening, readiness and openness. **(BDB)**

Ego and the organization influence one another.
Different organizational stages require different
types of egos. **(SJ)**

Ego is like an internal compass that helps you
lead with intuition. **(MV)**

Ego makes you come across as self-assured and
creates the perception of managerial courage,
stimulating others to follow you. **(MH)**

Ego makes you work from integrity
and affability. **(LVG)**

EGO CAN PROTECT US:

If there are difficult decisions to be made, my ego
helps me to not sacrifice too many of my own needs
for the common good. This helps reduce the risk
of burn- or bore-out. **(AVP)**

It asks a lot of energy to protect
your self-image. **(JK)**

Ego drives me to protect myself,
to establish limits in my own interest. **(ME)**

My ego protects me, (un)consciously,
from being hurt. **(IGo)**

EGO CAN ENGENDER TRUST AND SELF-LOVE:

The ego helps you to recognize your own
vulnerability and to be more trusting. **(LVG)**

You can make your ego subordinate to who
you are fundamentally. **(LdV)**

The ego is the ultimate externalization of I,
it is about self-love: I love me! We can only
love others if we love ourselves. **(BDB)**

CONNECTION

The ego helps us to contact other people's egos,
which is very important in conflict situations.
If you present yourself as equal to others,
it can provide new ideas. This can stimulate
new ways of thinking and it can help us to
integrate into groups. People are herd animals.
Loners can't survive. **(IGo)**

The ego hinders real cooperation by making it difficult to
find common ground. This is especially true for dominant
egos; the ecosystem is influenced by them. **(SJ)**

EGO CAN PROMOTE AWARENESS:

The ego can have a positive effect if we are aware of
our strengths and weaknesses and show this. **(HW)**

The ego is neutral. Ego can be a good thing,
for example when it helps us to be of service to others.
Ego can also make you selfish, which is, of course,
a disadvantage. **(TL)**

The ego is powerful and destructive. **(NB)**

The ego is about awareness of our vulnerability
but also of our capacity to trust. **(BDB)**

Ego inhibits authentic behavior. Ego connects
with others for strategic reasons, it hinders us from
being ourselves. **(ME)**

Self-awareness means understanding how your
ego affects you and this helps you to discipline yourself
in a positive way. You seek validation of how you see
yourself. **(TS)**

Survival strategy helps. Ego is about balancing
my different parts. Some parts are invisible; that is
what I should work on. **(DA)**

Ego is the source of charisma, consciousness
(of our competencies), it helps us to be disciplined,
it contributes to vanity. **(JMD)**

EGO OBSTRUCTS WHEN YOU FEEL FEARFUL:

On the one hand, the loud ego encourages you to
avoid fear and discomfort and on the other,
to satisfy needs. The ego can hinder you when
you need a lot of confirmation. **(BDB)**

Ego drives your need for recognition, to have the
right to participate. If recognition is lacking, you are
faced with a dilemma: do I accept this or do I leave
my comfort zone? **(MV)**

When entrepreneurs put a succession plan in
place and make difficult choices, they have to be able to relinquish control. Ego can prevent this through stubbornness
and inefficiency. **(MH)**

When an ego is just window dressing, it is negative and peo
ple will eventually see through it. **(IGe)**

Ego can get in the way when a person sticks to their opinion, while everyone else has a different view. **(TS)**

Ego behavior can undermine other people; you are taking pleasure when others fail or even helping them to fail. **(IGo)**

3

WHERE DOES EGO COME FROM AND WHAT DOES IT DO?

We want to take you on a trip through the landscape of human behavior. This landscape is found in the world of the ego. So, what is an ego? How do our egos motivate and influence our behavior? How do our egos evolve? How can we best explore and better understand our egos?

It is an inescapable fact that we all have an ego. Our ego underpins who we are, the part we call I. Your ego helps you to plan your day and to select and store memories. The ego directs how you respond to your experiences and form opinions about them. Your ego guides you in how to react to the world around you. Your ego is essential for you to function and, as such, it is part of being human, like a finely tuned instrument in the orchestra of your mind. The ego defines:

- How you see yourself: what is your self-image, your self-esteem?

- How you connect with others: how do you identify with others, develop connections, include or exclude others?
- How you deal with inner impulses: do you discipline yourself and modify impulses in an appropriate way?

Every human being has an ego. In other words, there are as many egos as there are people.

Your ego takes root in your infancy and evolves as you grow from dependent child into adulthood, experiencing the good and the bad events that make up your life. As a young child, you learn to simplify your experiences so they can be easily categorized and integrated. You develop a personalized overview of the human experience and refine your understanding of what is expected of you and how you can get what you need.

Seemingly insignificant events, when processed through the child mind, can have profound effects on your subconscious understanding, on your view of the world and your place in it. As children, we draw conclusions and beliefs and internalize them based on sometimes incomplete information. You conclude unconsciously: never do this again. Or: if I do this, my parents laugh and they love me. Sometimes these conclusions are incorrect. One man remembers: "As a seven-year-old, I was using a knife to remove the cover of the taillight on my bike when my father entered the room. He looked at me in shock and said, 'Why are you doing that with a knife?' I concluded from this that he didn't love me." This childish and mistakenly drawn conclusion became a prominent feature in the landscape of this man's ego and had disruptive consequences in his adult life. You conclude unconsciously: never do this again.

These key moments may be small, but are also fundamental. The influence of traumas on the development of a child can be significant. These influences, taken together, stimulate a child to make choices about what to show and what to draw back within themselves and which solution they choose in order to get what they want. This is how "frozen" aspects – the choices you are no longer aware of – are formed. On the other hand, you also form "strategic" aspects, which govern how you decide what behavior you show on the outside. These aspects are important for finding your place in the world. The frozen and strategic parts are connected with one another. The strategic parts hid your frozen parts from being visible. (Hans Knibbe calls this a split between the withdrawn and the strategic self in his handbook, *Being Orientated*).

This patchwork of behavioral strategies and the inner dynamics that are part of it develop across the course of your life to form a guide to the world as seen by your ego. Your guide provides you with certainty as a child, with a foundation. It determines what you perceive and how to interpret what you perceive and forms your individual frame of reference as an adult. Your guide tells you more about yourself than it does about the real world and makes it difficult for people to see you for who you really are. After all, you can only reveal to others those parts of yourself of which you are conscious. You cannot reveal your embedded parts.

The ongoing connection between your strategic and frozen "self" manifests itself in your behavior. As a child, your objective is to get what you need. We are dependent beings who have to learn how to interact with our environment in order to survive. We view others as objects that exist to help us get what we want. If they do not behave in ways that suit us, we protest. As we mature, we become independent, but our subconscious minds retain dependent impulses. This can create internal conflict as our need to be independent struggles against the habit of dependency.

The ego guides you through decision making and its consequences in daily life. Your guide helps you to decide what to say, what to think and how to react. It applies to only a part of the world because the frozen parts – those feelings and parts of yourself that you repressed in the past as you learned how to survive – are not included. Yet you stick to your guide because you have learned that this is the best way to avoid fear and anxiety. This is called the 'loud ego'.

The more familiar we become with our map of the ego's guidance, the more aware we become about how our ego influences our choices and behaviors. We become aware that our reactions are based on subconscious choices from our childhood. We realize that reality is much more complex and elusive than we had thought. This is both good news and bad news. The bad news is that we learn that much of what we thought was real is an illusion. Part of our frozen selves begins to thaw, a destabilizing process that causes anxiety, because we feel we are losing control. The good news is that our perspective becomes more attuned to reality and that our perspective evolves as our ego develops.

The more we learn to manage and develop our ego, the less we are at its mercy. Instead, we learn to use our ego to work for us, to be at our service. This is what we call the quiet ego. It is characterized by:

- An unprejudiced consciousness
- An inclusive identity (a feeling of being connected to the world)
- A compassionate self-identity
- An equilibrium between attention for yourself and others
- Oriented towards growth and development.

A comparison of characteristics of both the loud and the quiet ego can be found in the next table.

CHARACTERISTICS OF THE LOUD AND THE QUIET EGO

LOUD EGO	QUIET EGO
• Oriented towards self, more than towards others	• Listens to others
• Seeks to confirm one's own perceptions and has faith in them	• Inner and outer world
	• Self-aware, conscious of own behavior
• Unaware of one's own positive and negative characteristics	• Compassionate
• Corresponds with ego	• Doesn't correspond with ego
• Self-serving, strives to serve own interests	• Open, transparent behavior
• Defensive behavior	• Not prejudiced about oneself and others
• Overt focus on avoiding fear and discomfort	• Feels connected with the world
• Few meaningful connections with others, narcissistic	

In Chapter 5, the loud ego is presented in more detail. The quiet ego is presented in Chapter 8.

4

TWO PERSPECTIVES: I AND WE

Now that we have explored the world of the ego or "I", we are ready to consider the "We" perspective in the context of the workplace. The stages of development from I- to We-perspectives, and their eventual coalescence, form the basis of our model for how organizations can improve efficiency and workplace environments. We-perspectives are important because they create the environment within which the I-perspective functions. Stated otherwise, We-perspectives are a determining factor in how our egos are manifested. I- and We-perspectives cannot be considered independently because they are interdependent.

THE I-PERSPECTIVE – THE INDIVIDUAL

Every change we have to deal with requires us to alter how we observe things and how we think about what we see. In chapter 3, we learned that our perceptions and how we interpret them have helped us to simplify our view of the world from an early age. It is difficult, if not impossible, for the individual to put their views into perspective. The challenge and the key to evolving our ego is to realize and to accept that our view is one of many interpretations, that our view of reality is relative and transient. This requires a flexible ego, because our ego tries to keep us within existing and known perceptions. In order to develop as an individual, to develop our I-perspective, we need to become aware of our ego: who we are, who our authentic selves are.

Attempts to affect organizational change often fail on an individual level because our ego automatically guides us back to former, familiar behaviors as a defense mechanism. Change can cripple us on an individual level and repress our creativity, making it all the more difficult for us to accept the complexities of reality. The process of change can be made easier if it is done hand-in-hand with work on developing a better awareness of our egos and the defense mechanisms that our ego oversees.

THE WE-PERSPECTIVE - THE ORGANIZATION

The organization does not exist on its own; it exists only through individuals. When people connect and collaborate on common goals, the organization is formed. The organization's perspective is therefore the We-perspective. Groups of individuals react differently from individuals. A lack of interpersonal connection between members of groups, as is increasingly common in modern-day organizations, can lead to an atmosphere of "mental absence": people become isolated, work becomes boring and people begin to feel vulnerable. This hinders the development of self-awareness and creativity and, ultimately, hinders the business process.

Organizational change programs succeed only if the behavior and attitude of its individual members change. The next table summarizes some important features of successful change programs.

CONDITIONS THAT FACILITATE ORGANIZATIONAL CHANGE

CONDITION	BENEFIT
• Improve manager's/leader's social skills	• Better able to rally support from general staff
• Space for reflection and contemplation	• Become self-aware, realistic and authentic
• Behavioral changes by managers and staff	• New behaviors prevent reverting to type
• Responsibility for change is shared	• Encourages a sense of ownership, commitment
• Responsibility for managing ourselves	• Improves self-esteem, dignity, buy-in and ego-development

We have found distinct parallels, in our client work, between the development of the ego, "I", and the development of the organization, "We", as summarized in the table on the next page. The development of I and We is an iterative process. The fact that individuals adapt to change and develop at different rates makes the process of organizational change highly dynamic. In fact, change becomes a constant element in healthy organizations.

STAGES OF I AND WE DEVELOPMENT WITHIN ORGANIZATIONS

	I	WE
1	**LOUD EGO** • We respond to childish impulses	**FORMING** • We operate individually and in isolation with limited cohesion and cooperation
2	**EGO-AWARENESS** • We begin to recognize our ego and its facets • We request feedback	**STORMING** • Individuals begin to interact, react and collide, the concept of We begins to take root, we start giving feedback to colleagues
3	**EGO-MANAGEMENT** • We learn through iterative interactions how to adapt our behavior	**NORMING** • New norms, interconnectedness and interdependence emerge
4	**EMERGENCE OF THE QUIET EGO** • Inclusive • Empathic • Emotionally engaged	**PERFORMING** • New social contract • Authentic behaviors
5	**SPIRIT**	**WHOLENESS**

The five developmental stages of I, the ego:

1. **Loud ego** - We focus on ourselves, paying little attention to our environment and the consequences of our behavior.

2. **Ego-awareness** – The beginnings of self-awareness or consciousness. What is the source of my motivation? What energizes me? What demotivates me, blocks me? What am I afraid of? We start to question our behavior and its effects on others. We become interested in feedback on our behavior and actively seek it out.

3. **Ego-management** – We begin to manage our ego, a difficult task which our ego resists, because management means that we touch upon our vulnerabilities. Persistence and sustained motivation are required at this stage. We must be compassionate about ourselves as our imperfections are revealed.

4. **The quiet ego begins to emerge** – Our efforts in the previous stages have created room for different behaviors that are considerate of our environments. Our perspectives of ourselves and the world around us becomes less prejudiced, more inclusive and empathetic.

5. Spirit – We become aware of the most deeply embedded aspects of our identities. Our spirits are present when we are born. We look for ways to use this
all-containing stage to further evolve and enhance
our ego.

SCHEMATIC REPRESENTATION OF THE I-PERSPECTIVE

SPIRIT

EGO-DEVELOPMENT
TOWARDS THE QUIET EGO

EGO-MANAGEMENT

EGO-AWARENESS

I AND THE LOUD EGO

The five developmental stages of We, the organization:

1. We work in isolation, without much cohesion or co-operation with colleagues. Such organizations are often top-down driven. Our boss tells us what to do and with whom to do it, but we are only occasionally successful. Cooperative projects are hampered by colliding personalities and power struggles that are denied or ignored. Such organizations are perpetually in what is known as the team forming stage. Productive teams cannot form in companies that remain at this stage.

2. Teams form but their members soon become frustrated by a lack of cooperation and cohesion in the team and in the organization and begin to discuss it. These conditions offer an opportunity for change. Some may dare to endure conflicts if given sufficient encouragement that it will eventually lead to operational improvements. The phase is also called the storming phase. (Psychologist Dr. Bruce Tuckman differentiates four phases in team development: forming, storming, norming and performing). Feedback sessions are useful in such situations to help team members become conscious of their behavior and its effects. Group analysis to identify organizational inefficiencies can also be helpful at this stage.

3. Team members are becoming aware of their behavior and its consequences. It becomes easier to discuss conflicts and to agree on solutions. There are open and ongoing discussions about how to become more efficient. These conditions allow for discussion and exploration on how to achieve further efficiency and apply co-creation.

4. Teams collaborate with all stakeholders to identify and follow highly collaborative and efficient routes towards success. Responsibility in the organization is more equally spread across a networked organization and individuals self-organize. This allows the members of the organization to consider, together, a new social contract to embrace more than only basic conditions for a good workplace.

5. Wholeness – Many emerging companies and some that are long-established strive to reach this stage, in which the organization is not limited to its concrete activities in support of its business model. Responsibility and power are shared differently. The organization becomes an eco-system where making profit is a condition that is a product of a more important objective – striving for happiness. (See Frederic Laloux, *Reinventing Organizations,* Nelson Parker, 2014.)

SCHEMATIC REPRESENTATION
OF THE WE-PERSPECTIVE

WHOLENESS

SELF-ORGANIZATION – NEW
SOCIAL CONTRACT – PERFORMING

CO-CREATION – NORMING

FEEDBACK CYCLES
STORMING

WE AND FORMING

In the following chapters, we discuss stages of "I" and "We" in more detail.

5

CHARACTERISTICS OF THE LOUD EGO IN ORGANIZATIONS

In this chapter, we describe the first stage of our model. The I is unaware and incompetent. For We, this is the forming stage.

I-PERSPECTIVE

SPIRIT

EGO-DEVELOPMENT TOWARDS THE QUIET EGO

EGO-MANAGEMENT

EGO-AWARENESS

I AND THE LOUD EGO

STAGE 1 – THE LOUD EGO: UNAWARE AND INCOMPETENT

We now explore more deeply the dynamics of our ego. If we followed only our instincts, like other animals, we would remain the playthings of our ego. We would have no choice but to assume the identity and behaviors dictated by it as infants and children, assuming such behaviors were crucial for survival. We respond to body sensations, thoughts and feelings impulsively through directions that arise from our subconscious.

The loud ego is the foundation stage in the development of the ego. The loud ego manages itself based on its simplified map of the world to provide security in complex environments. (See Chapter 3). Each of us displays the loud ego from time to time in response to various contexts, for example, in response to stimuli encountered in organizational environments. Loud egos have some common characteristics. In this chapter, we present a number of methods for recognizing the loud ego in the workplace.

SIMPLIFICATION

The ego simplifies what it detects to avoid dealing with the complexities of reality. It sorts through input and selects a few recognizable details, a subjective selection, to form a simple representation of the world. This black-and-white thinking often arises in stressful situations.

> Reacting stubbornly,
> inability to listen. (**MH**)

MASKS

The loud ego never reveals itself completely. It is afraid of being visible. The loud ego masks its frozen part to reveal its strategic part. Masking the ego's frozen part enables its strategic part to fit into team norms rather than to stand out. The loud ego works behind the scenes to detect what is appropriate or expected in a given context. As a consequence of the unconscious activity of our ego directing our behavior, colleagues are prevented from seeing our true identities. This phenomenon often occurs during the first months of employment and can form and distort our position and development within organizations.

Some people are really into themselves, egocentric. **(SVU)**

You need to pull off your mask, to show your vulnerability
to provide connection. That is something I do consciously.
It is important to be conscious about your own behavior.
That is how you can influence others. **(ME)**

PLEASURE AND DISCONTENT

Creatures focus on what nourishes them in order to
survive. We humans are drawn towards good food, hav-
ing fun, things that attract us in some way, to what we
enjoy. We call this the pursuit of pleasure. In contrast,
some things repel us or disturb us in some way so we
avoid them. We will refer to this as the avoidance of
discontent. Much of our behavior is determined by this
phenomenon without us noticing it. Both pleasure and
discontent are characterized by the avoidance of real
connection.

People who find titles important, or do business
in their own interest without agreement. **(LVG)**

OFFENSE

Offense is caused by injury or humiliation. Offense often arises in response to being ignored or overlooked, or when the desires of our egos are unfulfilled, or when our needs are not satisfied. We can also be offended when our pride or honor has been damaged. This category of unmet needs is not critical for survival, but they have a strong influence on our behavior.

> We look for recognition, from relevant
> people, that matches our idealized self-image. (IGo)

BROADCASTING

Communication is about broadcasting and receiving. The loud ego prefers broadcasting. It assumes that the receiver will follow the message or that it can be convinced to do so. In terms of contact and connection, this is not a good strategy, as many receivers will not feel that they themselves have been heard.

> The "too big" ego, unaware of its blind spots,
> makes people out of step with reality. (AVP)

People who are unwilling to listen, who attack
immediately, who ridicule others, who think
they are better than everyone else. **(BDB)**

DEFENSE

The loud ego is egocentric and eager to preserve and
strengthen its identity. It is essentially a survival system,
a defensive mechanism. It perceives the world and its
people as potentially threatening. New things are not
accepted and are perceived as dangerous. The ego reacts
to what is new and unknown defensively in a manner
that protects its own interests.

Egotistic people impose their thoughts on others,
they will not yield nor admit mistakes, leading sometimes
to manipulation or abuse of power. **(JMD)**

DECISIVENESS

The loud ego behaves decisively in order to distinguish
itself. It is I driven, not reacting to others. Ego, in fact,
can help to get things done.

Ego drive can help to meet objectives,
to overcome obstacles. **(MH)**

As a board member, I see leadership, vision and guts as
a trinity. My ego is not important, I don't put myself in the
middle. The vision (dream) is the focal point; whatever the
consequences, you must be ready to lose your job. **(LdV)**

RECOGNITION

Recognition is crucial for a child's development; it helps
to build a basis from which to reach the next developmental steps. Subconsciously, our ego continues to
seek recognition and we become disappointed when we
do not get it. This is a childish orientation that is best
replaced by a more adult form of mutual recognition,
leading to better interpersonal contact and cooperation.

I speak up for myself, at the right moment,
to get the recognition I want. **(TS)**

WE-PERSPECTIVE

WE STAGE 1 FORMING: UNAWARE, INCOMPETENT

We recall from Chapter 4 that at the first stage of We-development, individuals work on their own; there is not much cohesion or cooperation. In this stage teams and organizations are inefficient and/or full of conflicts. Employees perceive one another as competitors rather than collaborators, or they don't even think of others at all. They work from 9-5 and do not want to be bothered by difficult questions.

People work to earn a living but also because, as social animals, we enjoy being part of something. But people at stage one of We-development see their team as an island of individuals and do not care much about one another, the environment, or clients. Employees are simply production tools. Their human potential is underused and this underused potential is often seen as a threat by management. Management is top-down, dictating the company's structure and steering the organization. People are dependent on the leader.

As a consequence, employees are not motivated to take responsibility. They are fixated on their own tasks and they have little understanding of the objectives and functions of the whole organization. Appreciation is given by management when the main tasks are well done. This is all that is asked of employees, nothing more. People working at this stage usually feel a strong separation between work and private life.

6

EGO-AWARENESS:
I BEGINS TO CONSIDER WE

In this chapter, we describe the second stage of our model of development, the stage when I becomes aware of the ego and its role in making choices and determining behavior. This awareness propels We into the storming phase.

I-PERSPECTIVE

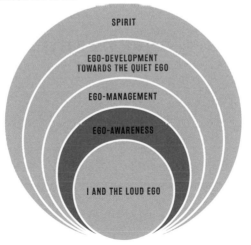

SPIRIT

EGO-DEVELOPMENT
TOWARDS THE QUIET EGO

EGO-MANAGEMENT

EGO-AWARENESS

I AND THE LOUD EGO

Ego is behavior related to emotions. The ego is programmed
like left-handed writing. People do need self-knowledge
to accept the image and the impact the ego has
on emotions. **(IGo)**

Issues dealt with at this stage are: understanding your emotional responses, how to make more conscious choices rather than being driven by subconscious impulses, how all of this will help you to be better at determining and controlling your behavior.

Becoming ego-aware allows you to progress to ego-management and finally to ego-enhancement. This is an iterative process that requires much reflection.

Nickolas Martin distinguishes three main components of the ego (*The Ego Unmasked: Meeting the Greatest Challenge of Your Life*, Dorrance, 2010):

- Ego-size
- Ego-permeability
- Ego-fragility

Each of these components plays a role in ego-related behaviors where the relative size of each individual's components defines an ego-type. The following questions, drawn from Martin's book, can help you get to know these components of your ego. Which questions resonate most for you or do you identify with most? Your answers help to define your ego type. We recommend that you review your answers to these questions with members of your environment.

EGO-SIZE

The most extensively studied ego component is ego-size: Those with an overly large ego-size usually have an amplified need to control, dominate and influence other people.

QUESTIONS RELATED TO EGO-SIZE

1. How much input do you attempt to provide in your environment?
2. How easy or difficult is it for you to be less responsible or to let other people do things for you?
3. How important is achievement to you?
4. What level of achievement do you expect to reach?
5. In relationships, what do you do more or less: take, share or give control to your partner?
6. How high is your self-esteem?
7. Do you manage change or does change manage you?
8. How often do you find yourself in conflict with others?

EGO-PERMEABILITY

This component determines how well we are able to develop and grow. People with low ego-permeability have developed their own opinions/self-image and hold on to them with great tenacity. They seek new observations that confirm their opinion. People with high ego-permeability are more flexible. They incorporate external input into their opinions. Some people are highly influenced by outside input. It is an art to distinguish by what or whom you choose to be influenced.

QUESTIONS RELATED TO EGO-PERMEABILITY

1. How willing are you to listen to and learn from significant people in your life?
2. How open are you to new ideas and choices and from whom?
3. How much respect do you have for your own knowledge and your capacity to think?
4. How tolerant are you of people who are different from you? Do you often spend time with them?
5. How well can you tell the difference between people you should and shouldn't listen to?

EGO-FRAGILITY

Everybody reacts differently to stressful events, like setbacks, fights or too many stimuli at the same time. Some people can ignore these things, while for others they cause a severe distraction. Some have a need to talk about what stresses them. This doesn't mean that one person has more (physiological) stress than another, nor that one reaction is better than another. The point is to acquire a better understanding of your ego-fragility and where or how you could modify your reaction.

QUESTIONS RELATED TO EGO-FRAGILITY

1. How easily do you become upset when confronted with the changes that occur in your life?
2. How easily do you become upset when confronted with adversity?
3. How long do you stay upset when confronted with a specific stressor (argument, financial setback, etc.)?
4. Do you tend to over/under react to anger/anxiety?
5. Do you find yourself feeling anxious/angry without specific reasons?
6. Do you find it difficult to feel emotions?

When we get to know these three ego components better, and their relative weight or contribution to the nature of our ego, we are making progress on the path to ego-awareness.

WE-PERSPECTIVE

We have now reached the second stage of We development: storming. Organizations often get stuck at this stage, because it is at this stage that employees become dissatisfied with the organization's lack of flexibility and innovation. Something must be done to enable the organization to respond to internal and external requirements. It may be time for behavioral changes by management. Members of the organization as a whole recognize the necessity for better cooperation and individuals start to form teams and to work together. This can lead to collisions, misunderstandings and differences of opinion revealing strains in the fabric of the organization that remained under the surface during the forming phase.

In some organizations, it is important to just be present and observe. One has to be aware of ego-driven behavior for it to be used positively. **(TS)**

Hostility, passive cooperation and many other emotions can be present during the storming stage, creating a tumultuous atmosphere. Additionally, the manager who has come up with the overall plan for organizational change will be challenged. Individuals and teams will become polarized, a necessary first step towards eventual development. We typically see that resistance to tasks, requirements and rules occurs. These challenges occur because there is a tendency for some to revert to former behaviors before the new norms for cooperation have taken root in the organization.

CONNECTED LEARNING

This situation calls for management to provide guidelines that clarify its vision for the direction the organization will take. This will distract employees and cause turmoil, anxiety and uncertainty. Such situations enable us to recognize one another's positive intentions, especially when management encourages all participants to have a sense of responsibility to find the solution. Conflicts can be discussed and we can learn to give and to ask for feedback. There are methods that help individuals and teams to resolve conflicts without being judgmental, creating more openness and opportunities for learning. These situations are also ripe for introducing further team development sessions. During the process, it is important to celebrate small steps and to minimize the impact of mistakes and disappointments. Management of expectations is important to enable employees to be aware of possible outcomes. During this phase, the connection between the Board, management and employees will be evolving. A first understanding of the We-perspective will be created. Leaders guiding the process need to know themselves and their ego well; they should be one step ahead in the developmental process.

The environment is important for ego-awareness;
the manager is responsible for creating it by delegating
correctly – with control – in order to get results:
participative management. Make sure there are many
challenges from which people can learn a lot. **(MH)**

I prompt my teams to work together, randomly composed
and also with external partners (business world).
I am looking for hybrid teachers. I see teams as an
ecosystem with diversity and durability. **(SJ)**

CULTURE

A company's organizational culture functions like its
ego and is developed without conscious thought. Leaders in an organization play an important role in creating
a culture. If they have big egos, or are authoritarian,
hierarchically oriented and share little information, a
different culture will be developed than in an organization where much is shared and self-organization is
stimulated. Culture influences employees' behavior.

In the last 3 years we have gone through intense
cultural change going on, led by the new CEO, towards
more customer focus. This is time consuming, as
we are learning new competences, a new language and
feedback about our behavior. We stick too much to
old hierarchical behavior. **(HW)**

PARTICIPATIVE LEADERSHIP

For participative leadership, it is important to delegate
and control without micro-management. Some managers are incapable of managing without overseeing de-
tailed activities. This is often the case with managers
who have grown from a technical background and who
lack social skills.

Our leaders lack maturity, they are really technically
oriented with a lack of passion for people.
Dual leadership can help; one leading the people,
the other, the technical part. **(RV)**

An organization can develop consciousness by encouraging managers to help people to understand the mission of the company: why do we work here together? People increase their belief in the importance of working together, how to take responsibility and how to provide constructive feedback.

We have more managers than leaders, with some exceptions because we don't take enough time to train these people correctly in the much-needed social skills. (MV)

If people are not yet ready, because of distrust or because they are not used to giving each other feedback openly, confrontation is possible. Managers need to lead from the front, in the open, providing an environment of openness and trust.

A CEO who provides time and space is in contrast with someone who is leading from his office only, because he is too self-absorbed. (HW)

It is often useful to involve employees in strategy development, but questionnaires can also be used to gauge views on, for example, the organization's climate, job satisfaction and stress levels. When outcomes are shared and key indicator results discussed openly, management creates common ground for collective organizational improvement, especially when this is done in mixed groups, with members of different teams.

As a leader, you have to show you can really listen and give people something back, which they might have overlooked. You will get a lot back. This is especially helpful for uncertain people. (MV)

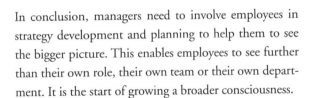

In conclusion, managers need to involve employees in strategy development and planning to help them to see the bigger picture. This enables employees to see further than their own role, their own team or their own department. It is the start of growing a broader consciousness.

The optimal context is one that stimulates you to give the best of yourself, believe in yourself, dare to fix things. This implies that the number of rules should be reduced to a minimum. (JMD)

7

EGO-MANAGEMENT: FROM I TO WE

After developing your ego-awareness, you can begin to start managing your ego. This is the third stage of the model where your authentic self begins to guide your ego. The presence of colleagues with skills in ego-management causes the transition of We to the norming development stage.

I-PERSPECTIVE

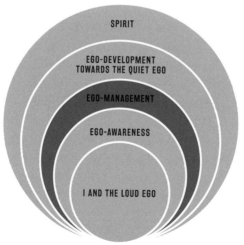

SPIRIT

EGO-DEVELOPMENT
TOWARDS THE QUIET EGO

EGO-MANAGEMENT

EGO-AWARENESS

I AND THE LOUD EGO

In chapter 6, we learned about how an understanding of three components of your ego help you to become more ego-aware. They are:

- Ego-size
- Ego-permeability
- Ego-fragility

It is a mistake to think that an organization will improve when/if each individual within it optimizes the balance of these components within their own psyches. This is illusory thinking. Achieving equilibrium with and between everyone would require that everyone became the same and this would have the effect of reducing the creative potential within the organization. What you can do is to address how knowledge about the balance between your own ego-components can help you to manage your ego.

When a situation is annoying, irritating or boring, you can choose how to react. You can choose to make your ego serve your wishes: in other words, you can manage your ego, making it an instrument of your deepest will.

Egos have to be controlled by building in checkpoints, which are checked carefully with others and updated if we are performing as we need to. A person's character can inhibit their ability to develop their ego. A risk averse person will find it difficult to develop their ego. **(MH)**

An example: someone with high ego-fragility has well-developed antennae, making them very sensitive to the atmosphere and health of the organization. Like a canary in a coal mine that is susceptible to even minimal increases in carbon monoxide, an ego-fragile person can sense strains within an organization and sound an alert before a problem brings it to a standstill. These people are often seen as weak or oversensitive, instead of being recognized for their valuable skills of perception.

Some people don't have enough ego; you have to stimulate them. Dare to give them feedback about this. Ego behavior is also showing emotions and sometimes crossing limits. **(LVG)**

The lesson to draw from this is that your goal is not to develop in a linear sense but in a dynamic and interactive manner: to acknowledge issues, to meet, to discuss and to connect. When this happens, it means the next step in developing the We has arrived. Taking this step is itself an early intervention into the existing culture (which will be discussed in Chapter 8).

EGO-SIZE

The bigger the ego, the more opposing force you need to achieve development of consciousness. People with a big ego can have more or less connection with the outside world. If there is a lot of connection, it is possible to stage a session with members of the team aimed at contradicting the perceptions of the person with the big ego. People who have a large ego are strongly driven from within and are bad at accepting contradictions (low permeability). Additionally, integration into teams is difficult for them, because they have an overt need for compliments and shows of appreciation. It is important to first mitigate this need before subjecting them to a contradiction session.

Mitigate the need to bestow compliments and shows of appreciation on people with a big ego by helping them to:
- Become more open to external signals
- Organize objections
- Learn to decrease the need for acknowledgement
- Allow others to influence relationships
- Understand the power that comes from being less controlling

People with a small ego may also have problems with ego-development. As they are less visible in organizations, it can be difficult for them to accomplish goals. Such people need to learn how to become visible. This may make them uncomfortable but they can be motivated to try it if they are given opportunities to understand how fulfilling visibility can be when it is linked to achievement.

Some people exaggerate and overdo things.
Some people blame their failures on others and attribute their successes to themselves. For people with small egos, the reverse is true. **(IGo)**

People who want to grow their ego can be helped by:
- Understanding that controlling their life is important
- Understanding that lack of control in relations has a negative impact
- Learning to take independent decisions
- Learning to voice objections

EGO-PERMEABILITY

People who have low ego-permeability are not easily influenced by others and by their ideas. This makes working together and change processes difficult, which sometimes results in them being ignored. Their interpersonal skills may be poor, while the content of their arguments and ideas are sound. The challenge is to help them overcome their difficulties collaborating while increasing the transmission of their valuable ideas and content.

People can grow their ego-permeability by:
- Considering the opinions of others
- Learning to make compromises
- In discussions, not only talking but also really listening to others
- Understanding that decisions need support

Open leadership is very important. As a leader, you have to know your people and their private situations, but you have to keep this information to yourself. Be discreet. I have always been interested in the drivers of people, and of clients. (IGo)

People with a high permeability ego allow themselves to be overly influenced by the environment. They benefit from learning to be more self-oriented and to express their opinions. This allows them to stand stronger. It requires a process of empowerment, including learning to object to things they disagree with.

People appreciate it if we listen well. I was too open: for me "less is more" is a motto. (HW)

People can lower their ego-permeability by:
- Embracing their uncertainty or doubt as a quality
- Taking themselves and their opinions seriously
- Asserting their right to be heard as well as to listen
- Guarding their limits, if needed

EGO-FRAGILITY

When you have high ego-fragility, you are very conscious of your own and others' feelings. Others may perceive this as a weakness, when in fact, you can be particularly perceptive, which is a valuable trait. Ego-fragile people are often encumbered by inner noise or pressure when trying to share their observations and ideas at the right time and in a manner that the listener will accept. The alternative is that you may choose to keep your observations and ideas to yourself.

Emotions are about connecting. This is important for you and for your ego. Cultural differences have a strong influence on how we deal with emotions. Look for example to the Netherlands compared to Belgium when we talk about showing emotions or to France compared to Britain. (AVP)

People with high ego-fragility can mediate this by:
- Understanding that they are not the same as their thoughts and emotions
- Applying self-leadership to steer their feelings and thoughts
- Learning to make a choice if and when to show their emotions

Emotions can become stronger than ego:
this can reduce, for example, our self-assuredness.
It helps if we can discuss them. (MH)

People with low ego-fragility are not aware of what is happening internally nor in their environment. In situations that demand cooperation, this can mean that people with low ego-fragility can be perceived as lacking in empathy, resulting in communication difficulties, for example.

People with low-ego fragility can become more effective team members by:

- Getting more in touch with their feelings and their subtle shades
- Appreciating that their feelings are part of who they are
- Learning to perceive and recognize the feelings of others

Emotions are the engine of acting; you can strengthen these either upwards or downwards. When I am anxious, I can talk about it, which is positive. I can also hide it and prepare myself for battle in order to survive. **(BDB)**

WE-PERSPECTIVE

WHOLENESS

SELF-ORGANIZATION –
NEW SOCIAL CONTRACT – PERFORMING

CO-CREATION – NORMING

FEEDBACK CYCLES
STORMING

WE AND FORMING

For the We-perspective – optimizing cooperation – we will work with others to find approaches to realize behavioral change. In this phase, the norming stage, the team will agree how to deal with one another and how best to work together.

The process starts with listing the topics and issues about which team members have different opinions. Unity of I and We appear when the differences between them are openly addressed and resolved, resulting in the development of cohesion and a deeper bond. During this process, it also becomes clear what is hindering cohesion and cooperation. The issues may need to be revisited and reviewed several times to find the right solutions and team members may need to be encouraged by leaders to persevere.

The We-perspective will reinvent itself as a result of this process. Employees will begin to realize that they have to collaborate to reach a higher target. Each incremental stage of the process is important and can energize the team as the targets are met. Group cohesion grows and people begin to discuss things more appreciatively and openly as task ownership conflicts diminish.

The process is steered by management; employees as well as managers have ownership of the process, and are responsible for fulfilling their roles. This requires connection within and between the layers of the organization, interactive teamwork and a reflective attitude by all participants. New situations will develop constantly and will need to be managed. Change agents and ambassadors will play an important role by translating change into practice and collecting information from practice for input to the next iteration.

> The dream we defined was important for coping and has influenced the whole transition process. (LdV)

For leaders, self-knowledge is important; their role changes from introducing ideas to coaching and facilitation. When the leader is not motivated to share and coach, the process often fails. Leaders should regularly communicate the status and progress of teams against their targets.

> It helps when you can add value in a coaching manner, not if you are just telling. You have to find the right balance between providing space and controlling. Dancing as a metaphor: don't step on each other's toes too often, don't be too pushy, let yourself lead too. (HW)

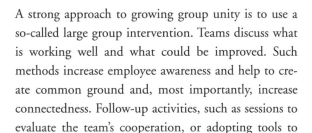

A strong approach to growing group unity is to use a so-called large group intervention. Teams discuss what is working well and what could be improved. Such methods increase employee awareness and help to create common ground and, most importantly, increase connectedness. Follow-up activities, such as sessions to evaluate the team's cooperation, or adopting tools to measure progress and provide feedback, are needed to maintain the health of and to further improve cooperation. (For more on these topics see *Co-Creation… 13 Myths Debunked,* of which Hans Begeer is co-author).

Create a mirroring environment that looks for interaction, for example feedback about meetings. The leader should dare to be vulnerable, developing a feedback culture based on real values and steps. **(MV)**

SHARED OWNERSHIP

In a situation of shared leadership, dominant leaders can hinder working together as equals. Old forms of authority need to be reviewed; a potential group discussion can be implemented: what is working together equally about? How do we work equally in an organization with hierarchical roles, in which decisions are already made? This implies that the decision-making process needs to change, where the decision maker understands and is influenced by different angles and perspectives from employees.

The effect of this is more maturity, more social dynamics and responsibility. Employees become participants with more autonomy and a better understanding of the bigger picture. **(RH)**

During the process of shared ownership, everybody has a duty to take an active role and responsibility. For this to happen, these questions are important:

- Has everybody contributed?
- Has there been enough listening?
- Have there been enough continuing questions?
- Were the differences described and recognized in a positive way?
- Were enough ideas summarized and did people have a chance to react to them?
- Have difficult complaints been solved?

Working together equally leads to a safer working climate. It means everybody can define their limits, feeling free to make mistakes, without being judged negatively, but instead leading to open discussion. Every employee becomes more visible; anonymity is slowly neutralized.

You have to manage, to control your ego, for instance,
by introducing a feedback culture. **(HW)**

DIVERSITY

In the We-perspective, permeability is important for influencing others and being influenced yourself. This requires you to make choices in cooperation, using your understanding that you are working to a united goal. Everybody feels better heard, recognized and connected with the We-perspective. Also, there is room for more creative thinking and for abandoning your own image of how things should be.

It appears to be very difficult to make people look neutrally
or objectively; their opinion is too strong. You have to help
them to check their own ego. **(AVP)**

When we are clear and transparent about the desired diversity within the We-perspective, we identify differences and the objective is to use them. For example, during meetings the chairman chooses a method that allows different opinions to be expressed, such as:

- Brainstorming, without disapproving of ideas
- Silent wall discussions, people writing their ideas without discussion
- Mixed subgroups
- Rotating chairmanship

The chairman encourages learning by summarizing, asking questions, pointing out differences, taking no strong stand and working towards a common agreement in which the differences are appreciated.

An organization should embrace diversity. People have the right to be themselves. It is an obligation to discuss behavior, which is more difficult than discussing work results. For me, an open culture is essential. This asks for much discussion, workshops, exemplary behavior and repetition. **(IGo)**

INTERNALLY AND EXTERNALLY ORIENTED

During this stage, we also look for and allow the opinion of external stakeholders. These can be clients, network partners or knowledge institutes. By asking and listening to their opinions, a deepening form of cooperation develops.

VIEW ON WHAT IS GOING ON

Ego-fragile people transmit important information, such as whether everybody was heard enough and whether some issues increase tension. It is important that the We-perspective embraces employees with high ego-fragility and doesn't ignore them. Often, these people are not liked. Too much sympathy leads to pampering, too little to isolation. Both reactions influence ego-fragility negatively. People with low ego-fragility miss these kinds of signals, but the We-perspective can appeal to such people, helping them to grow their understanding of what goes on in themselves and other people.

> My ego helps me to help others when they are in trouble.
> I stand up for my people and protect the weaker ones.
> I notice it is difficult to provide people with genuine and
> authentic feedback although they need this to grow. **(LV6)**

8

EGO AND ORGANIZATION DEVELOPMENT

During the fourth phase of our developmental model, we are more aware of our egos and better at managing our behavior, developing a quiet ego. We begin to perform from the We-perspective.

I-PERSPECTIVE

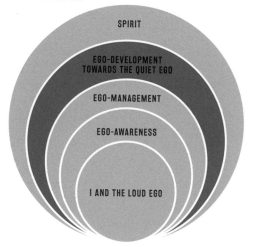

SPIRIT

EGO-DEVELOPMENT
TOWARDS THE QUIET EGO

EGO-MANAGEMENT

EGO-AWARENESS

I AND THE LOUD EGO

How do we continue to transform our ego into an instrument that enables even further development? This requires an inner attitude through which you neither lead by desire (what you like), nor by discomfort (what you don't like). So you try to operate from a position between the two extremes, from which you are capable of objectivity and free of biases. You may even become wise.

During this phase of ego-development, you become aware of your needs and take responsibility for them. Consequently, you are able to overcome impulsive behavior. You have a clear state of mind. For example: "I always want to have the last word, but now I understand that this irritates my colleagues. I have tried to control this behavior in the past and failed. Now I can manage it."

During this phase of ego-development, you don't decide if you do or don't like something. Instead, you are open to ideas in an unprejudiced way. You allow your creative forces to drive your behavior rather than by making ego-driven choices. You shape yourself, not from your ego as a guide, but from your authentic self as a guide.

We arrive at a stage that we can describe as the quiet ego. We have an inclusive identity, in which there is a feeling of connectedness with everything and everybody. You can focus more easily on the environment and feel part of it without losing your identity. Your internal and external motivation is in balance, which allows you to have a less defensive and more integrated attitude.

> I force myself to look for new opinions and to ask questions to which I do not know the answers. This requires a fit ego. It requires vulnerability and guts. (AVP)

The quiet ego is colorful, clear, fit and has a strong will. Clearness translates into the ability to differentiate between the meaningful and the senseless and to act on the distinction. In this way, the quiet ego is passionate, lively and alert.

The quiet ego also has an empathic perspective and wants to grow, to develop and to deploy what it learns. This results in a more joyous and satisfied life. The quiet ego is characterized by self-compassion, which leads to self-acceptance; you like yourself and appreciate your contributions. It identifies realistic life goals, which you can influence yourself more easily. The quiet ego accepts that you are not perfect and shows itself to be vulnerable in a healthy manner.

People help me by providing feedback. I ask questions and really listen. This is how we develop our mind. It is a luxury to work in an environment of appreciative understanding. **(SVU)**

WE-PERSPECTIVE

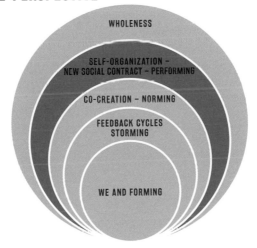

During the previous stages, we developed our consciousness towards a We-perspective. The We-perspective is a separate identity, a body standing on its own that needs to develop itself further. But it fits everybody, like a glove.

We always run our teams like we are in a relay race. We use each other's complementary abilities; it is not always the same person running in front. People have to stop using "I"; it is about "We". **(IGe)**

For the We-perspective to function as an identity, it is important that all behaviors contribute to the unit, the We. This doesn't mean that everybody is doing the same, as each individual has their own preferences. But commitment is needed to develop the unit as a whole, with the potential for everyone to contribute. Leaders need to clearly explain and encourage this concept.

We are undertaking an important transformation towards more self-organization. This requires authentic leadership, openness, honesty and transparency. **(LVG)**

The We-perspective monitors whether employees serve the higher goal. This is a part of a learning organization. A mutual understanding of this objective and an agreement that this is what an organization wants to achieve creates a sort of social contract that allows the We-perspective to function as an entity.

SOCIAL CONTRACT

The social contract can be described as an exchange between the organization (We) and the employee (I). The agreements within the social contract are based on group values and support the kind of organization the participants want it to be. It is about matching the needs of people with the organization; the I and the We. The social contract specifies how we work together (e.g. behavior, communication, treatment of one another, learning together, enhancing one another's development). It describes how the We wants to be – for everyone. New employees are selected based on how they fit the criteria and whether they will commit to it.

There is a range of thoughts about how we treat
one another; this is written down. It forms an important
part of designing a vision. We always talk with each other,
not about each other. During conflict, we engage in
dialogue and work towards a common result. There has to
be a hygienic way to make decisions in an open, emphatical
and vigorous way. **(RH)**

NEEDS

Often, needs are described using three levels, following
Alderfer, who improved Maslow's model. But we see the
need for a fourth level. On the level of the quiet ego
and corresponding organizational cooperation, there is
a need for an integrated view and spiritual attention. I
and We are intertwined on this level.

ELEMENTS OF A SOCIAL CONTRACT

MATCHING	I, THE INDIVIDUAL ASKS FOR:	WE, THE ORGANIZATION ASKS FOR:
• Existential needs	• Income and support • Safety and security	• Labor • Physical and mental performance • Effort, adaptability
• Social needs	• Belonging to something • Social contacts • We-feeling, inclusion	• Cooperation • Connection • Loyalty • Identification, pride
• Developmental needs	• Ego-awareness • Ego-management • Ego-development	• Inventiveness • Creativity • Flexibility • Proactiveness
• Need for integration and spirituality	• Meaning something for the whole: the organization, the socio-economic and ecological systems • Connecting with the spirit	• Spiritual presence • Ego serves We • Focusing on the whole, a joint creation

As a leader, I want to connect around a goal,
with a unified way of working, under one flag. **(MV)**

CONTINUAL CHANGE

We understand that change is a never-ending process. The only certainty is that the environment is constantly changing. By discussing strategic and inter-disciplinary themes, the organization develops the flexibility to change too. A focus on learning enables people to exchange their roles and tasks to fit the evolving needs of the company. Employees who no longer fit their role can be helped by feedback, so that they can develop other skills and in time look for another job inside or outside the organization.

Other changes may include:
- Employees become attracted to and responsible for We; a feeling of ownership of the organization is formed.
- The border between work and private life slowly vanishes; employers become interested in the views of employees outside the work environment and may be influenced by them.
- Silence rooms can be provided for reflection or prayer.
- Meetings can begin with a reminder of the organization's values.
- The organization can offer training programs or courses focused on personal development.

STRUCTURE: FLATTERY AND SELF-ORGANIZATION

During this stage of our model, the concept of working together for better results has become the group norm. A maintenance program is needed to continually fine-tune the organization and to overcome inevitable setbacks. A new open and sharing climate develops. We are on our way to becoming an organization that embraces and grows from continual change – a learning organization.

Ego-development requires openness; asking people to participate in complex decision making and showing your vulnerability helps. **(MH)**

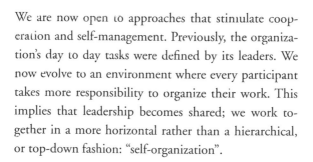

We are now open to approaches that stimulate cooperation and self-management. Previously, the organization's day to day tasks were defined by its leaders. We now evolve to an environment where every participant takes more responsibility to organize their work. This implies that leadership becomes shared; we work together in a more horizontal rather than a hierarchical, or top-down fashion: "self-organization".

Organizations need to encourage self-management,
to offer coaching, to discuss progress of work and life
with their employees. There has to be a win-win situation
for both the individual and the organization. **(RV)**

CO-CREATION

Learning organizations proactively seek methods that improve collaboration. One example is co-creation. This is a management method that helps participants to appreciate the opinions of their colleagues and to discover the benefits of self-management and shared responsibility. Representatives of the whole organization's environment, including clients where it is practical, work together to solve complex issues. Some aspects of co-creation are:

- The group designs the way forward together to ensure efficiency and commitment.
- Meetings are managed and responsibility for their management is shared by rotating the roles of meeting leader, time-keeper, secretary and presenter.
- We look for what unites us, for points of agreement rather than disagreement, and act on this.
- We nurture diversity of opinions, innovation and creativity.

By introducing such methods, people learn how to listen to others and not just to themselves. You discover the power of self-management and responsibility. By working in a co-creative way, you can fine-tune the way you work to achieve the results you are aiming for, and you can agree to measure performance along the way. Everyone shares responsibility for team-performance.

Trust is basic – without this, we fail. We have to be open, show interest, ask questions and show respect. In our diverse world, this can be difficult as there are cultures in which this is quite different from how we do it in the West. (SVU)

9

BEYOND I AND WE:
SPIRIT AND WHOLENESS

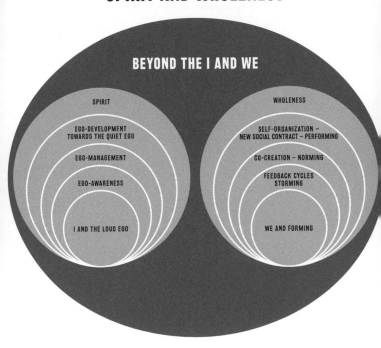

BEYOND THE I AND WE

SPIRIT

EGO-DEVELOPMENT
TOWARDS THE QUIET EGO

EGO-MANAGEMENT

EGO-AWARENESS

I AND THE LOUD EGO

WHOLENESS

SELF-ORGANIZATION –
NEW SOCIAL CONTRACT – PERFORMING

CO-CREATION – NORMING

FEEDBACK CYCLES
STORMING

WE AND FORMING

I- AND WE-PERPECTIVES

Spirit is the stage at which everything is connected; there is always connection and there is always communication. We no longer distinguish between I and We and we move as a unit, as a relationship. We form spirit from the ego, where the ego serves the spirit. This is who we are at our deepest level; the spirit inspires us to use our wisdom and translate the impulses of our ego into behaviors that can be used in everyday life. This process is continual. In Buddhism, this is called an ego-free state, which is timeless, free of judgement, open and affectionate. We can use visualization and meditation techniques to contact our inner sources of wisdom. We need to let go of our ego as a point of orientation and no longer identify ourselves with our ego for this to happen.

EXERCISES TO RELEASE US FROM IDENTIFICATION WITH EGO

1. Take a comfortable seat. Focus your attention internally. Concentrate on your breathing. If a thought or feeling arises, let it pass by like a cloud in the sky. You don't have to do anything with it. You return your attention to your respiration.

2. During the day, take a moment to think about what is going on within you. Tell yourself you are not your thoughts, nor your feelings. You have them but you are not them. You observe the thoughts and feelings, you become an observer; this can incite surprise, confusion or aversion. Deal with it, as in exercise 1.

3. When you encounter fierce emotions, take a moment to observe them (exercise 2). You take the inner decision to explore what this emotion is doing to you. When you have gained some insight into the emotion, let go of it. Tune in to your quiet ego and decide to act based on wisdom.

4. Reflect on those moments in life when you were busy attaching to people or things or states of mind and consider how they fed your ego and how you saw yourself, how they affected your identity. With continued practice, you will release yourself from these things and express your authentic self.

Continuous practicing is required to let go of your identification with ego.

On this level of spirit, nothing is proscribed, nothing is fixed; there is permanent movement, there are no polarities. This is the most fluid and unconstrained stage of the model. Your ego can become quite defensive at this stage as you remove the security it formerly provided. Yet if you persevere, you find that at this stage there are no limits to further development, your horizons are open. By releasing everything, an endless space develops that provides new possibilities and releases creativity. You are in the now, where your thinking is clear, centered and compassionate.

The organization is open, a network organization, which pays attention to the whole. It is a prerequisite to make profit, but not the most important one – striving for happiness is more important. An organization striving for happiness wants its employees to be healthy psychologically and for the employees to strive for client satisfaction. In this way, the lifeblood of both the people and the organization is strengthened.

(10)

CASE STUDY: VIATTENCE

In 2014, Laurent de Vries was invited to join the board of directors of Viattence, a Dutch nursing home that was in ill-health financially. His mission was to return Viattence to operational and financial health.

At the start of this process, the organization was characterized by low levels of cohesiveness and cooperation, which De Vries believed was the source of its poor financial performance. He was clear about his vision for leadership: he knew that he had to be aware of his ego as a leader to avoid hindering the organization. He saw his ego as subordinate to organizational goals. For the first year, he simply listened. He met with employees in all functions and at all levels. He asked many questions about what they liked and disliked and especially about their passions. In the first year, he connected broadly with the employees. He believed it was important to establish these connections before introducing changes.

At the end of the first year, he formulated a vision: within five years, he wanted Viattence to be the best nursing home in the Netherlands in terms of patient care and financial performance. He chose 60 people he recognized as informal leaders or early adopters and met with them regularly to agree on a vision for the organization and a plan for achieving it. The planning process helped to identify who would and would not be best suited to being a member of the envisioned organization, resulting in some people leaving the organization voluntarily.

The Viattence vision involved a paradigm shift from a medical model to a human oriented model, in which the well-being of the clients and the staff was central. This made it clear what kind of organization Viattence wanted to be and what type of We-perspective the organization needed to adopt to make this possible. The We-perspective helped to define the organizational, facility and human resource needs, as well as the required quality of leadership and the financial resources needed to support all of this. The We-perspective was the point of departure and everything was oriented around making it happen. Employees became owners of the solutions and the Viattence mission was founded: perceive the human being.

Examples of the actions taken were:
- Asked stakeholders to support the vision
- Revised the facility to fit clients' needs
- Organized feedback cycles using a method called Images of Quality
- Adapted work processes to the human oriented model
- Adapted employee training to this model
- Agreed on how to treat clients and how to collaborate to achieve this
- Developed a lifestyle program for employees
- Adopted management styles to fit the model
- Critically reviewed all protocols, resulting in omitting 380 of 480 protocols.

CASE INTERPRETATION

De Vries initiated the entire process of change from the position of a quiet ego. This, in combination with his work experience and vision, allowed him to perceive the potential of the organization and its employees. He implemented connection, starting at stage 1 (the forming phase) by just listening and mirroring during the first year, using himself as a vehicle for identifying change requirements.

Development of the We-perspective was realized by formulating the vision and presenting a business case that underlined the financial need for change. This encouraged buy-in and support from the I-perspective egos in the group. This stimulated many debates during which people were asked to listen to one another and to appreciate their differences (ego-size, ego-permeability, ego-fragility). During this (storming) stage, the I-perspective evolved, leading some people to look for new jobs while the commitment of others to the organization increased.

This second stage was supported by feedback cycles, using the Images of Quality method. This helped to make people aware of their attitude and behavior towards clients and colleagues, leading to changes in I- and We-perspectives. This provided space for changes on I and the We levels, because there was no judgement involved.

New approaches were, where feasible and practical, written down (part of the norming stage). Employees were encouraged to take ownership of the changes. This required willpower and ego-management from management and employees.

This process supported the continued development of the I- and We-perspectives. Ego-management drove people to We and the I was carried to the next stages. Within a few years, the organization reached the performance phase and great gains were made in the quality of life of clients and in profitability. This proved that the transfer of more responsibility to employees, and putting their egos at the service of clients worked; this approach allowed the organization to meet its goals. The employees had achieved connection and reached a spiritual stage of performance that continues to today. The development never stops.

(11)

SUMMARY AND CONCLUSIONS

Everyone has an ego: organizations include as many egos as there are employees. In our quest for a better life and more efficient organizations, we limit ourselves to either the individual I-perspective, or the organizational We-perspective most of the time. In this publication, we connected the two perspectives. We distinguished five developmental stages and we discussed both the I-perspective and the We-perspective at each stage.

The first stage is the basis we build upon: one is unaware and incompetent. The I perspective lacks introspection. It does not ask itself many questions about drivers and behavior. In organizations, we tend to work from nine to five. We act as required without asking if and how this can be improved. This is the level of the loud ego (the I-perspective) and the forming stage (the We-perspective).

At the second stage, one is more aware but still incapable. The I-perspective asks itself why it reacts as it does and what effect its behavior has on others. Something similar happens in the We-perspective: how can we work together more efficiently, and how can we work in a more interesting way, with more pleasure? Ego-size, ego-permeability and ego-fragility are the three main components of the ego and it is through self-reflection on how these aspects of your ego help and hinder collaborations that you can evolve your ego and become more productive. It is important to organize non-judgmental feedback processes that can help to initiate and sustain learning capacity. This is a difficult process, because changes can lead to discontent and conflicts. That is why this is called the storming phase in models of cooperation.

The third stage involves acquiring skills for ego-management, where you are more aware of your own ego and behavior; you try to guide the ego and evade traps. This requires conscious and competent behavior, while you regularly fall back to less competent behavior. In the We-perspective, we call this the norming phase: together, we try to come to agreements about more efficient and conspicuous cooperation.

At the fourth stage, the ego evolves into a quiet ego. The I-perspective becomes more in balance with that of others and people behave more inclusively and empathetically towards others and towards themselves. Feedback is seen as an opportunity to learn, which supports further development of the organization. Self-organization and self-management are possible and even necessary approaches, enabling employees to work together more efficiently, resulting in greater satisfaction and happiness. The result is better performance.

The fifth stage is that of soul and spirit. From the We-perspective, we speak about wholeness. During this stage, the I- and We-perspectives are connected, forging a networked organization with attention paid to all stakeholders. We work not only for profit but for the whole ecosystem, and we want to contribute to it. We are capable yet unaware because we don't need to think about how to best behave. The I- and We-perspectives are merged.

(12)

HOW THIS BOOK CAN BE
OF HELP TO YOU

This publication can serve you on both the I- and the We- levels. It can help you to start thinking about your ego and your behavior.

Ask yourself this, if you haven't already done so while reading: at which stage of development is your ego? Has it been at the same stage throughout your life? You can use the questions from chapter 6 to increase your self-knowledge. You can ask people you trust for feedback on these different themes. Choose people with different views or experience. Our advice is to ask yourself these questions frequently, for example, when you are in the midst of a difficult situation or if you have recently realized a success.

You may uncover insights by realizing how you perceive your own behavior. Consider imagining yourself behaving differently, then try it out and assess the results. Be easy on yourself and be aware that it takes a lifetime learning process to realize the potential of the process.

The point is to step out of your map that has been defined by your ego more often, to take a broader view. It is part of the course that you will fall back into old habits and impulsive responses that arise from your ego. The aim is not necessarily to divorce yourself from your ego, but rather to understand what you are doing in the world of your ego and to step back out of it. Taking a broader perspective leads to more productive analyses of the situations you encounter. By perceiving your loud ego and that of others, you create an optimum distance to reflect and make choices that let you manage your ego and behave differently.

You can decide how your behavior is influenced by the context, for example, by the organization and by the group dynamics. Which coping strategies should you choose? After this has become clearer, you are able to replace your impulse-driven behavior with free choice. With your widening view, you aim for the potential of yourself and others. You will only be able to see these if you release your ego-map. You start to perceive the connection between things. This leads to positive expectations that affect both you and your environment. Now you can apply ego-management in order to get to your view. Positive expectations about yourself have a bigger impact on your behavior than negative ones.

To work on the I-perspective means also working on the We-perspective and vice versa.

Being a manager in an organization has implications, as the described ego-development is important: you are a role-model for others. Your vision determines the direction the organization moves in and what you see says something not only about your organization but also about yourself. Our advice is to look at your organization with a view of wholeness and potential. This provides space. Perceive and accept that everything is constantly changing. Be a role model, be vulnerable, be accessible and organize objection. In the We-perspective, apply positive expectations using the enlarged view.

Think about which context is needed to take the first step. The start of this requires formulating a common vision. By applying co-creation, you can involve all stakeholders in this process. This has consequences for decision making: it requires equality at all levels.

Self-management and self-organization are then applicable. You can only use these methods if you have changed your own role and relate it to your own development.

It is important to organize feedback at all levels. Feedback processes are often perceived negatively and incite anxiety. Therefore, we advise you to choose an appreciative approach, as in the case illustrated in chapter 10. Developing self-leadership for all participants is important and also helps them develop their ego.

Make sure there is enough diversity on all levels. Think about men/women, introverts/extroverts, thinkers/doers. For healthy group dynamics, you need to explicitly appreciate diversity and, as a leader, to take responsibility especially when the going gets tough.

Step by step, a different social contract evolves. You can leave this implicit, or where needed you can confirm and formalize it. A community and a community feeling evolve. You can strengthen this with an infrastructure that supports the community and by common activities and a social intranet, with space for both business-related and private messages. This will result in more satisfaction for employees, more creativity and innovative power, which in general lead to better performance.

As previously mentioned, your development as a leader is crucial. Our advice is to start a process to get to know yourself better. You can't do this on your own; your own map will hinder you and this is true for everybody.

We wish you great success with your developmental journey.

ABOUT THE AUTHORS

Hans Begeer (1957) is an occupational and organizational psychologist and a self-employed management consultant. He has written several books about his extensive professional experience, like *Co-creation is… 13 Myths Debunked*, as a co-author; and as author, *Doe-het-zelf-leiders – De hiërarchie voorbij: Praktijkboek voor zelforganisatie*. For Begeer, *Ego@WORK* forms the logical continuation of his previous publications.

He is preoccupied with the question of how it is possible that people say they want to relinquish control, but are unable to do so. And the answer is the ego hinders the application of real self-organization. In his consulting practice, Hans applies the concepts and methods that are also described in this book. He strives to help people to develop themselves further and to make organizations nicer and better places to work.

See www.bmc-consultancy.be for more information.

Roel Reitzema (1953) is counselor and trainer/coach. He is trained in humanist and Buddhist psychology. He advises companies and trains employees in self-assessment, communication and cooperation. Also, he works with individuals on existential questions.

In his profession, he focuses on the development of consciousness: the aim is to transform yourself into the form closest to who you truly are. He works systemically as every human being is connected with the environment: you influence and are influenced. During sound cooperation, this is in balance. He looks for wisdom interrelated with feelings and thoughts and ways to express these. This could mean helping stagnating teams, increasing individual work satisfaction or improving communication between different layers of the organization.

See www.coaching-training.nu for more information.

PRAISE

"I see more and more organizations pretending to work on symbioses between I and We, applying official value charters and colorful slogans on a daily basis. The intentions are genuine enough! But at the same time, I perceive a louder cry from employees for another type of social contract. The annual employee satisfaction survey no longer seems to touch us; it is in its last gasp and the time to set it aside is rapidly approaching.

Imagine that together we were able to experience our organizations as ecosystems in which we could be or, better yet, would be the best version of ourselves. This sounds utopian, so we prefer to stick to the existing formulas to the end.

Hans Begeer and Roel Reitzema rise to the challenge and peel the onion in their publication *Ego@WORK*. From a clear analysis of what takes I and me to We and us, Hans and Roel postulate both a humbling and hopeful message: it starts with our ego and the readiness to really work together with all the other egos in the organization. This means muddling through the discomfort, being different, and the not yet voiced, towards newly agreed engagements and most certainly new forms of organizational structures.

The "higher me" and the "higher we" are characterized by the ability to release, and to let go. Do we dare? It is the choice of each individual as to how closely he wants to approach this ideal though after going through this compact book, the reader will realize there is no option but to act on these insights. The authors provide an accessible frame of reference to work on yourself and on your organization. On top of this, readers of Hans's *Co-creation... 13 Myths Debunked* and *Doe-het-zelf leiders* will find a perfect fit with previously described themes. Get to work on your ego!"

Marc Verbruggen | General Manager Novartis – Puurs site

"Successful, innovative and lasting entrepreneurship asks for awareness of I and We, serving the company process. *Ego@WORK* presents a thinking model that helps you to relate to behavior, leading and facilitating it towards desired development within your company."

Just Smit | Entrepreneur, founding father and shareholder of Adimec

"Too often ego is seen as something negative. It hinders you if you need much confirmation. But the positive ego is about authenticity and being autonomous with full respect for yourself and others. This book helps you to develop the positive side of your ego."

Bart De Bondt | CEO YouthStart Belgium and CEO teamdebondt

"This book teaches you that ego is not something negative. It allows you to learn to know your unique I and use it to get the desired organizational culture."
Saskia Van Uffelen | Digital Champion Belgium

"This book dares to discuss a difficult subject like ego. In modern management this is much needed: at either extreme, too little ego results in a lack of entrepreneurship, while too much ego seriously hinders optimal cooperation. The book is instructive and easy to read. It provides insights on the concept of ego, and offers practical methods to manage ego and to help it evolve. What makes this book even more special is that it accounts for the fact that every individual is part of an organization and if the individual is evolving, the organization has to evolve too. For both, a synchronized approach is presented. The book is clearly based on practical experience and provides enriching evidence and many insights."
Marc Heeren | Board Member and Business Consultant

"A clearly presented guide that enlightens an often-misunderstood concept. Ego gives you power and colors your personality. Acknowledging and applying this authentically during times of uncertainty connects and provides meaning."
Ann Van de Perre | Executive coach / ICF PCC Marshall Goldsmith – owner of Annspired

"*Ego@WORK* invites you to become more aware of your leadership style and how it affects others. It provides clear insights and offers opportunities to adjust yourself. It is a must read to reach a stimulating We culture for which we all long and which will diminish burn-out."

Hilde Wampers | Group Tax Director, Proximus

"Your ego or self-estimation is the way you present yourself in life. People with a big ego possess obvious charisma, positive self-assessment, strong discipline and unpretentious vanity. The book *Ego@WORK* presents a vision that leans heavily on this."

Jean-Marie Dedecker | Politician

WORD OF THANKS

For the interviews:
Bart De Bondt (BDB), Jean-Marie Dedecker (JMD), Ann Van de Perre (AVP), Luc Van Gorp (LVG), Marc Heeren (MH), Tine Slaedts (TS), Saskia Van Uffelen (SVU), Hilde Wampers (HW), Rita Verreydt (RV), Inge Geerdens (IGe), Ingrid Gonnissen (IGo), Marc Verbruggen (MV), Jan Kroes (JK), Jeannette van de Born (JvdB), Rogier Huffnagels (RH), Saartje Janssen (SJ), Laurent de Vries (LdV), Ton Leeggangers (TL), Daan Andriessen (DA), Noëmie Bezemer (NB), Michael Eichelsheim (ME).

For the use of the case study:
Laurent de Vries and employees of Viattence.

For reading critically and providing feedback:
Marc Verbruggen, Marc Heeren, Carla Derijck, Christine Reitzema, Tosca Hummeling, Just Smit and Ans van Belzen.

For proper coordination and publishing:
The team at LannooCampus.

For translation to English and the poem:
Lynn Butler.